HOW TO

OVERCOME

BAD

MEMORIES

:MEMORIES THAT HAUNTS YOUR LIFE

Major Prophet PD John
P.O. BOX 4016
Mwanza - Tanzania
Phone number:
+255 762 415 790/ +255 759 204 744
Yohanayona3@gmail.com
www.hlcentre.info

ISBN : 9798328304900
First edition ©2024.
Imprint: Independently published

Chief Editor:
Josia pd John
josiajohn735@gmail.com
Dar es salaam - Tanzania
Tel: +255 758588127/ +255 693522834

Dedication

To all those who have been haunted by their past, May this book serve as a guiding light on your journey to overcome the shadows of bad memories.

May you find solace and strength within these pages, and may you emerge from the darkness with a renewed sense of hope and healing.

This book is dedicated to your courage and resilience in facing your inner demons.

May you find peace and freedom on your path to overcoming bad memories.

Preface

We all have memories that haunt us. They linger in the depths of our minds, popping up unexpectedly and casting shadows on our present lives. These bad memories can torment us, affecting our relationships, self-esteem, and overall well-being. But there is hope.

In this book, we will explore the power of overcoming bad memories from a Christian perspective. We will journey together, discovering the transformative effect that forgiveness, Scripture, prayer, and community support can have on our healing process. By delving into the depths of our painful memories, we will uncover the key to reclaiming our lives and walking in freedom.

I have written this book with a deep understanding of what it feels like to be haunted by memories. Like many, I have wrestled with the pain, shame, and regret that comes from recalling past experiences that shaped me in negative ways. But through my faith and the guidance of the Holy Spirit, I have discovered that we don't have to be imprisoned by our past.

This book is not a quick fix or a magic solution. Overcoming bad memories takes time, effort, and vulnerability. It requires us to confront the pain head-on and be willing to go through the healing process. But I assure you, the journey is worth it.

Throughout the pages of this book, you will find biblical teachings, practical advice, and personal stories of individuals who have triumphed over their bad memories. Their stories serve as beacons of hope, reminding us that no matter how dark our memories may be, there is light at the end of the tunnel.

I invite you to embark on this journey with an open heart and a willingness to face your fears. Together, let's step towards healing and reclaim the abundant life that God intended for us. May the pages that follow provide you with comfort, guidance, and the tools you need to overcome the memories that haunt your life.

In His Grace,

[Prophet PD John]

My Testimony

In 2012, my world was shattered when a boy confessed to me that he had used witchcraft to kill my young brother. The weight of his words was crushing, and I felt my heart ache with a pain that seemed never-ending. Forgiveness felt like an impossible feat, and the memories of that moment haunted me day and night.

I found myself plagued with heart problems, both physically and emotionally. The bitterness and anger consumed me, leaving me trapped in a cycle of despair. It seemed like there was no escape from the darkness that clouded my mind.

But in my darkest hour, I turned to prayer. I begged God for the strength to forgive, to release the burden of anger that weighed me down. And in a moment of divine intervention, I received a vision. I was instructed to take a bicycle from my shop and give it to the boy who had confessed to killing my brother.

At first, I couldn't believe that it was truly a message from God. How could I offer kindness to someone who had caused me so much pain? But as the days passed, the message grew stronger in my heart. Finally, I made the decision to follow God's guidance and offer an act of forgiveness and compassion to the boy.

When I arrived at his home with the bicycle, I was met with tears and pleas for mercy. The boy confessed his sins, his guilt pouring out in a torrent of regret. Through his tears, he renounced the witchcraft that had consumed him and begged for forgiveness. His wife, too, wept at the realization of the pain they had caused.

In that moment of vulnerability and repentance, I saw the power of forgiveness at work. The boy and his wife surrendered their lives to Jesus, acknowledging the wrongs they had committed and seeking redemption in the arms of the true God.

It was a moment of profound transformation, a testament to the healing power of forgiveness and grace. Through my act of kindness and obedience to God's call, lives were changed, and hearts were turned towards the light.

In the end, I learned that true healing comes not from holding onto anger and resentment, but from releasing those burdens and offering forgiveness. And in that act of forgiveness, I found peace and freedom from the chains of bad memories that had haunted me for so long.

Table of Contents

Chapter I.

Introduction

The Power of Memories

Memories hold an incredible power over our lives. They have the ability to transport us back in time, to relive moments of joy, love, and laughter. Conversely, they can also bring us face to face with painful experiences that haunt us. The intricate workings of our minds can sometimes make bad memories feel as vivid and real as if they were happening all over again.

For example, Sara vividly remembers the day her father walked out on her family when she was just a child. That memory is etched in her mind like a scar, causing her to doubt her worth and struggle with trust in relationships. Another example is Mark, who carries the weight of a traumatic event he experienced in his teenage years. The memory of that event still triggers panic attacks and makes it difficult for him to engage in everyday activities.

Not only do bad memories affect our emotional well-being, but they can also have physiological effects on our bodies. The stress response triggered by these memories can lead to increased heart rate, elevated blood pressure, and even physical pain.

Importance of Addressing and Overcoming Bad Memories

Recognizing the importance of addressing and overcoming bad memories is the first step towards healing. Ignoring or burying them deep within us may provide temporary relief, but the memories will continue to exert their influence in subtle and destructive ways.

A pivotal aspect of addressing bad memories is understanding that we were not meant to carry the burdens of our past alone. God desires to walk with us through the healing process, offering comfort and restoration. He invites us to cast our worries and hurts upon Him, trusting that He will bring beauty from ashes.

In *Matthew 11:28-30,* Jesus says, *"Come to me, all you who are weary and burdened, and I will give you rest. Take my yoke upon you and learn from me, for I am gentle and humble in heart, and you will find rest for your souls. For my yoke is easy and my burden is light."* These words remind us that our healing journey is not intended to be traveled alone. God offers us rest and restoration as we entrust our pain to Him.

Book Clarification

It is important to clarify that this book is written from a Christian perspective. Our faith provides a unique lens through which we can view and overcome our bad memories. While the principles and strategies discussed in this book may resonate with individuals from diverse backgrounds, we believe that true and lasting healing is found in a relationship with Jesus Christ.

The Bible is replete with stories of individuals who faced their pasts, confronted their memories, and found redemption and restoration. Joseph, for instance, experienced horrendous betrayal by his brothers but ultimately forgave them and rose to a position of power. Peter, who denied Jesus three times, found forgiveness and a renewed purpose in serving the early church.

Throughout this book, we will draw upon these biblical narratives to shed light on the power of forgiveness, renewal of the mind, and relying on God's strength and guidance. When we overlay our experiences with the truths from God's Word, we find a solid foundation upon which to build our healing journey.

In the next chapters, we will explore the role of forgiveness in overcoming bad memories, the transformative power of renewing our minds through Scripture, seeking healing through prayer and worship, the significance of seeking professional help and community support, and ultimately, walking in freedom from our haunting memories.

Together, let us embark on this journey towards healing, knowing that our faith in God will guide us and lead us towards the restoration of our hearts and minds. May the words in this book serve as a source of encouragement, comfort, and practical guidance as we navigate the path towards overcoming bad memories.

Chapter II.

Understanding the Nature of Bad Memories

Definition of Bad Memories

Bad memories are the recollections of past experiences that bring about pain, distress, and emotional burden. They are often associated with traumatic events, hurtful words, or deep disappointments that have left a lasting impact on our lives.

For example, My brother Majaliwa carries the memory of being bullied throughout his school years. The hurtful words and actions of his peers have created feelings of unworthiness and inadequacy that still affect his self-esteem today. On the other hand, Michael recalls the car accident he witnessed as a child, which has bred a fear of driving and anxiety whenever he's behind the wheel.

How Bad Memories Affect Our Lives

Bad memories have a profound influence on various aspects of our lives. They can shape our belief systems, affect our relationships, and hinder our ability to experience joy and peace.

When we hold onto bad memories, they become lenses through which we view ourselves, others, and the world. Our self-perception can be distorted, leading to feelings of shame, anxiety, and fear. Additionally, these memories can impact our ability to trust others, resulting in difficulties forming and maintaining healthy relationships.

Recurrent bad memories can lead to rumination, where our thoughts continuously loop around the painful experiences. This cycle of rumination may heighten stress levels, disrupt sleep patterns, and compromise our overall physical and mental well-being.

Biblical Perspective on the Impact of Bad Memories

The Bible acknowledges the power and impact of memories on our lives. In **Isaiah 43:18-19,** God says, *"Forget the former things; do not dwell on the past. See, I am doing a new thing! Now it springs up; do you not perceive it? I am making a way in the wilderness and streams in the wasteland."* This passage reminds us of God's desire to free us from the grip of our past and lead us into a new and abundant life.

Furthermore, **Philippians 3:13-14** encourages us to *"forget what is behind and strain toward what is ahead...press on toward the goal to win the prize for which God has called me heavenward in Christ Jesus."* God wants us to move forward, allowing His redemptive power to transform our lives. He does not want us to be constantly burdened by the weight of our past mistakes, hurts, or traumatic experiences.

How Bad Memories Can Hinder Our Spiritual Growth

When we allow bad memories to consume us, they can hinder our spiritual growth and intimacy with God. These memories may cause us to doubt His love, provision, and faithfulness in our lives. We may struggle to fully surrender our pain to Him or trust His plans and purposes for us.

Moreover, bad memories can become stumbling blocks in our ability to forgive others and ourselves. Unforgiveness hinders our relationship with God, as Jesus taught in *Matthew 6:14-15,* *"For if you forgive other people when they sin against you, your heavenly Father will also forgive you. But if you do not forgive others their sins, your Father will not forgive your sins."*

By holding onto bad memories, we may find ourselves stuck in a cycle of bitterness, resentment, and anger, preventing us from experiencing the true freedom and peace that Christ offers.

In the upcoming chapters, we will explore the transformative power of forgiveness, renewing our minds through Scripture, seeking healing through prayer and worship, and the importance of seeking professional help and community support. By addressing these essential aspects, we can begin the journey of overcoming our bad memories and allowing God to guide us toward spiritual growth and restoration.

Chapter III.

Effects of Bad Memories

Living in Fear of the Past Memories

Living in fear of past memories is like being trapped in a never-ending nightmare. The constant replay of traumatic events or distressing experiences can create a toxic cycle that consumes our thoughts and emotions. It robs us of our peace, joy, and present moments. We are unable to move forward and instead remain bound by the grip of fear.

In the biblical narrative, we see an example of living in fear of the past memories in the story of Lot's wife. As Sodom and Gomorrah were destroyed, Lot's wife looked back, longing for the life she once had. In that moment, she was transformed into a pillar of salt, forever frozen in her past *(Genesis*

19:26). This cautionary tale reminds us of the dangers of dwelling on the past, as it can hinder our growth and keep us trapped in fear.

Testimony:

Sarah's Escape from Fear

My daughter in the Lord, Sarah was haunted by the memories of an abusive relationship she had escaped years ago. The fear and trauma continued to manifest in her daily life, making her fearful of forming new relationships and hindering her personal growth. I prayed for her and Organised Counselling Sessions, finally she was able to forgive her Ex- husband and moved on with her own life. Sarah learned to face her past, process her emotions, and break free from the paralyzing fear. She now lives a life full of hope and new beginnings, no longer shackled by the haunting memories of the past.

Causes Trauma

Bad memories have the potential to cause profound trauma within us. Trauma can result from experiences such as physical or emotional abuse, accidents, loss, or witnessing a traumatic event. These memories are deeply ingrained within our minds and bodies, often manifesting as anxiety, panic attacks, or even post-traumatic stress disorder (PTSD).

In the biblical book of Exodus, we encounter the Israelites who suffered under the slavery of the Egyptians for many years. Their memories of bondage and oppression caused immense trauma, affecting their ability to trust and live in freedom. Through divine intervention, God led them out of Egypt into the Promised Land, offering a path towards healing and restoration.

Testimony: James Journey to Healing

My Uncle James was a war veteran haunted by the traumatic memories of his time in combat. The sights, sounds, and emotions associated with war continued to plague him long after his return home, leading to debilitating anxiety and nightmares. With the help of therapy and support groups, James gradually learned to process his trauma and reframe his relationship with the memories. Today, he uses his experience to advocate for mental health support for veterans, offering hope to others seeking healing from their own traumatic memories.

Isolating Yourself from People - Loneliness

Bad memories can often lead to self-imposed isolation, where we distance ourselves from friends, family, and the community. We may fear judgment or rejection, believing that our past experiences make us unworthy of love and connection. As a result, we become trapped in a cycle of loneliness, further reinforcing the negative impact of these memories.

In the biblical story of the prodigal son *(Luke 15:11-32)*, the younger son's bad memories and shame led him to isolate himself from his family and community. He believed that his past mistakes were unforgivable and that he would be better off alone. However, through the unconditional love and forgiveness of his father, the prodigal son found the courage to return and rebuild his relationships.

Testimony:

My Release from Isolation

I was a survivor of domestic violence who had cut off all contact with my friends and family in fear of their judgment. This self-imposed isolation only intensified my feelings of shame and kept me from receiving the support I desperately needed. With the help of forgiving and letting go of the past, I began the journey of reconnecting with loved ones and rebuilding my social support system. The kindness and understanding I received shattered the walls of isolation, bringing forth healing and a renewed sense of belonging.

Causes Depression

The weight of bad memories can often lead to a deep sense of sadness and hopelessness, culminating in depression. The constant reliving of negative experiences, along with the accompanying emotions, can drain our energy and desire to engage with life. Depression takes hold, making it difficult to find joy, purpose, or motivation to move forward.

In the biblical narrative, we find the story of Job who experienced an unimaginable series of tragedies, losing his family, wealth, and health. The accumulation of bad memories left Job in a state of deep despair, questioning the purpose of his existence. However, through the restoration and divine intervention, Job eventually found hope and renewed strength *(Job 42:10-17)*.

Testimony: Paulina's Journey from Darkness to Light

My Daughter in the Lord Paulina struggled with depression, largely stemming from a traumatic childhood experience. The memories of the abuse she endured followed her into her adult life, making it challenging to find joy and meaning. I organised Prayers and Counseling Sessions and insured a strong support network for her. Paulina gradually learned coping strategies, reframed her relationship with the memories, and discovered a renewed purpose. Today, she advocates for mental health awareness and encourages others to seek help for their own battles with depression.

Psychological Effects

Bad memories can have a profound impact on our psychological well-being, leading to symptoms such as anxiety, low self-esteem, and distrust. These memories shape our beliefs about ourselves, others, and the world, often resulting in negative thought patterns and destructive behaviors.

In the Bible, we see an example of the psychological effects of bad memories in the story of Elijah. After experiencing a great victory against the prophets of Baal, Elijah was overcome by fear and depression, triggered by the threats of Queen Jezebel *(1 Kings 19:1-18).* His memories of persecution and the weight of his responsibilities overwhelmed him, leaving him vulnerable to negative psychological effects. However, through God's intervention and gentle guidance, Elijah found comfort and regained his strength.

Testimony:

My Transformation

I carried the burden of childhood trauma, which manifested in debilitating anxiety and low self-esteem. The memories of abuse led me to believe that I was unworthy of love and happiness. Through forgiveness and self-compassion exercises, I gradually challenged these negative beliefs and rewrote the narrative of my life. Today, I stand tall, thriving in personal and professional relationships, empowered by the transformation that overcoming bad memories has brought me.

Causes People to Give Up

When bad memories become overwhelming, one of the dangers we face is the temptation to give up. The weight of these memories can lead us to believe that there is no hope for a better future, convincing us that our efforts to move forward are futile.

In the biblical narrative, we find the story of the Israelites wandering in the wilderness for forty years *(Numbers 14:26-34)*. Their struggle to let go of the bad memories of slavery and embrace the promise of a new land caused them to give up and forfeit the countless blessings that awaited them. Yet, even in their moments of despair, God never left their side, providing manna and water to sustain them.

Testimony:

Godwin's Journey of Perseverance

My son in the Lord, Godwin battled addiction, a cycle perpetuated by chronic bad memories that left him feeling helpless and resigned to his circumstances. However, with the support of our

Prayer Group, We Organised a recovery program through Prayers and Counseling. Godwin embarked on a journey of perseverance. He fought against the grip of his memories, and although he faced setbacks along the way, he never gave up. Today, Godwin lives a life of sobriety and serves as a beacon of hope for others struggling with their own battles.

Causes People to be Judgmental

When we are haunted by bad memories, there is a tendency to inflict judgment upon ourselves and others. We carry the weight of guilt, shame, and resentment, projecting our own pain onto those around us. This leads to strained relationships, walls of separation, and a continued cycle of negativity.

In the biblical story of the woman caught in adultery *(John 8:1-11),* the memories of her past actions haunted her, leaving her vulnerable to public condemnation and judgment. However, Jesus challenged the crowd, inviting them to confront their own imperfections before casting judgment. Through his act of forgiveness and love, the woman was able to break free from the cycle of judgment, embracing a new beginning.

Testimony: Joyce's Redemption from Judgment

My daughter in the Lord Joyce carried the weight of an affair that had shattered the trust in her marriage and strained her relationship with her children. The memories of her actions left her consumed by guilt and self-condemnation. Through prayers, counselling and a commitment to rebuilding trust and connection, Joyce learned to forgive herself, ask for forgiveness from her loved ones, and ultimately let go of the cycle of judgment. Today, her family has grown stronger, bound together by a newfound compassion and a shared commitment to healing.

In conclusion, the effects of bad memories can be deeply impactful, shaping our thoughts, emotions, and behaviors. However, armed with an understanding of these effects and the tools for healing, we can reclaim our lives from the grasp of these haunting memories. Through the power of self-reflection, therapy, and the timeless wisdom found in biblical scriptures, we can break free from fear, trauma, isolation, depression, and judgment. Each testimony serves as a reminder that healing is possible, offering hope and encouragement for anyone seeking to overcome the grip of bad memories.

Chapter III.

The Role of Forgiveness

Forgiveness is a vital aspect of the healing process when it comes to overcoming bad memories. By forgiving ourselves and others, we release the burden of resentment, anger, and pain associated with these memories. Forgiveness allows us to let go of the past, make peace with what has happened, and move forward in our lives.

Understanding God's forgiveness and its significance

In this section, we will delve into the concept of God's forgiveness and its importance in the process of overcoming bad memories. We will explore biblical scriptures that highlight how God extends His forgiveness to those who seek it, emphasizing the transformative power of divine forgiveness in our lives.

Scripture Reference: *"If we confess our sins, he is faithful and just to forgive us our sins and to cleanse us from all unrighteousness." -* **1 John 1:9**

Steps to forgiving ourselves and others

In this section, we will outline practical steps to guide readers in the process of forgiving themselves and others. It is crucial to understand that forgiveness is a journey and not an event. We will provide practical tools and techniques to aid readers in this transformative process.

Scripture Reference: *"Then Peter came to Jesus and asked, 'Lord, how many times shall I forgive my brother or sister who sins against me? Up to seven times?' Jesus answered, 'I tell you, not seven times, but seventy-seven times.'" -* **Matthew 18:21-22**

Testimonies and real-life examples of forgiveness

To bring the concept of forgiveness to life, this section will showcase testimonies and real-life examples of individuals who have successfully overcome the impact of bad memories through forgiveness. These stories will serve as sources of inspiration and encouragement for readers, illustrating the transformative power of forgiveness in healing and moving forward.

Scripture Reference: "Get rid of all bitterness, rage and anger, brawling and slander, along with every form of malice. Be kind and compassionate to one another, forgiving each other, just as in Christ God forgave you." - Ephesians 4:31-32

Throughout this chapter, we aim to provide a comprehensive understanding of forgiveness and its role in overcoming bad memories. By exploring the significance of God's forgiveness, providing practical steps, and sharing real-life examples, readers will gain insight and inspiration on their path to forgiveness and healing.

Chapter IV.

Renewing the Mind through Scripture

The mind is a powerful tool that can either build or destroy a person's life. The thoughts that we entertain in our minds have the ability to shape our attitudes, actions, and behaviors. Therefore, it is crucial to guard our minds against negative thoughts and replace them with positive ones. One of the most effective ways of doing this is through reading and meditating on God's Word.

The Word of God is powerful and has the ability to penetrate deep into our hearts and transform our thoughts. *Hebrews 4:12* says, *"For the word of God is living and active, sharper than any two-edged sword, piercing to the division of soul and of spirit, of joints and of marrow, and discerning the thoughts and intentions of the heart."* When we read the Bible, we are not just reading a religious book, but we are reading the very words of God, which have the power to transform us from the inside out.

Identifying and replacing negative thought patterns

Negative thought patterns are like weeds that grow in the garden of our minds. They can take root and spread quickly if not identified and addressed. Negative thinking can lead to depression, anxiety, and other emotional and mental health issues. Therefore, it is essential to identify and replace these negative thought patterns with positive ones.

The Bible provides us with countless examples of how to overcome negative thinking. One of the most significant examples is found in **Philippians 4:8,** which says, *"Finally, brothers, whatever is true, whatever is honorable, whatever is just, whatever is pure, whatever is lovely, whatever is commendable, if there is any excellence, if there is anything worthy of praise, think about these things."* This verse gives us a blueprint for identifying and replacing negative thoughts with positive ones.

Daily affirmations and declarations based on God's Word

Daily affirmations and declarations based on God's Word are powerful tools that can help renew our minds and transform our lives. Positive affirmations are statements that we repeat to ourselves daily, which help reprogram our minds and replace negative thoughts with positive ones. Declarations are similar to affirmations but are more focused on speaking God's Word over our lives.

An example of a daily affirmation could be, *"I am loved by God, and He has a plan and a purpose for my life."* This statement reminds us of God's love for us and gives us hope and direction for our lives. An example of a declaration could be, *"I declare that I am healed by the stripes of Jesus."* This statement declares God's healing power over our lives and reinforces our faith in His ability to heal us.

Stories from the Bible that highlight overcoming bad memories

The Bible is full of stories of people who overcame bad memories. One of the most significant is the story of Joseph in the book of Genesis. Joseph was sold into slavery by his brothers and spent many years in prison before becoming the second in command in Egypt. Despite the hardships he faced, Joseph was able to overcome his bad memories and forgive his brothers.

Another example is found in the book of Nehemiah. Nehemiah was burdened by the destruction of Jerusalem and the exile of his people. He prayed and sought God's guidance, and with His help, he was able to lead the people in rebuilding the city walls. Despite the opposition he faced, Nehemiah was able to overcome his bad memories and accomplish God's purpose for his life.

In conclusion, renewing the mind through Scripture is the best way to overcome bad memories in your life. The Word of God has the power to transform our thoughts and replace negative thought patterns with positive ones. Daily affirmations and declarations based on God's Word are powerful tools that can help renew our minds and transform our lives. And, the Bible is full of stories of people who overcame bad memories, which serve as examples of how we too can overcome our pasts and live victorious lives.

Chapter V.
Seeking Healing through Prayer and Worship

The role of prayer in processing and releasing bad memories:

Prayer is a powerful tool in processing and releasing bad memories. Through prayer, we can bring our pain and burdens to God, expressing our deepest emotions and seeking comfort and guidance. In **Philippians 4:6-7,** the Apostle Paul encourages believers to bring their anxieties to God through prayer: *"Do not be anxious about anything, but in every situation, by prayer and petition, with thanksgiving, present your requests to God. And the peace of God, which transcends all understanding, will guard your hearts and your minds in Christ Jesus."*

When praying about bad memories, it is essential to surrender them completely to God, trusting in His ability to bring healing and restoration. By doing so, we acknowledge that we cannot overcome these memories on our own, but through God's strength and grace.

Encouragement to lean on God's strength during the healing process:

During the healing process, it is crucial to lean on God's strength. In *Isaiah 41:10,* God assures us, saying, *"So do not fear, for I am with you; do not be dismayed, for I am your God. I will strengthen you and help you; I will uphold you with my righteous right hand."* By relying on God, we find the strength to confront and overcome the pain associated with bad memories.

Through prayer, we can ask God to fill us with His peace and strength, enabling us to face our memories head-on. *Psalm 27:1* declares, *"The LORD is my light and my salvation—whom shall I fear? The LORD is the stronghold of my life—of whom shall I be afraid?"* This verse reminds us that with God by our side, we need not be afraid of the memories that haunt us.

Expressing emotions through worship and praise:

Worship and praise play a significant role in the healing process. When we engage in worship, we are actively focusing our hearts and minds on God, shifting our attention away from our pain. By expressing our emotions through worship and praise, we find release and connection with God's presence.

Psalm 107:28-30 beautifully illustrates the power of worship in the midst of distress: *"Then they cried out to the LORD in their trouble, and he brought them out of their distress. He stilled the storm to a whisper; the waves of the sea were hushed. They were glad when it grew calm, and he guided them to their desired haven."* Just as the psalmist cried out to the Lord in trouble, we too can find solace and healing through heartfelt worship.

Testimonies of individuals who found healing through prayer and worship:

Throughout history, countless individuals have found healing through prayer and worship. Their testimonies serve as reminders of God's faithfulness in redeeming and transforming lives. These testimonies can inspire and provide hope for those seeking healing from bad memories.

*One such example is the story of the Apostle Paul. In **2 Corinthians 12:7-10,** Paul shares how he pleaded with God to remove a **"thorn in his flesh."** Though God did not remove the thorn, Paul's understanding of God's grace and strength enabled him to find contentment and healing in his weakness. Paul's testimony encourages us to turn to God in prayer, trusting in His wisdom and sufficiency to heal our wounds.*

In conclusion, prayer and worship are powerful tools for overcoming bad memories. Through prayer, we process and release our pain, leaning on God's strength to guide us through the healing process. Expressing our emotions through worship and praise helps us find solace and connection with God. The testimonies of individuals, like the Apostle Paul, remind us of God's faithfulness and the transformative power of prayer and worship.

By incorporating these spiritual practices into our journey towards healing, we can find the strength, peace, and ultimately overcome the bad memories that haunt our lives.

Chapter VI.

Seeking Professional Help and Community Support

Recognizing when professional help is necessary is a crucial step in overcoming bad memories. While prayer and personal reflection are valuable, there are instances where seeking the expertise of a mental health professional becomes essential. This can be especially true when memories are deeply traumatic and negatively impact daily functioning, relationships, or overall well-being. Professional help can provide the necessary tools and guidance to navigate through the healing process.

Overview of therapeutic approaches for dealing with bad memories:

Therapeutic approaches offer a range of techniques to help individuals confront and heal from bad memories. Cognitive-behavioral therapy (CBT) focuses on changing thought patterns and behaviors associated with negative memories. Eye Movement Desensitization and Reprocessing (EMDR) is a specialized technique that helps process traumatic memories. Psychodynamic therapy delves into the unconscious to explore underlying causes of distress. These are just a few examples of the various therapeutic approaches available, and a mental health professional can determine which is most suitable for an individual's specific needs.

The importance of seeking support from fellow Christians:

In addition to professional help, seeking support from fellow Christians can play a significant role in the healing process. Christians who have gone through similar struggles can offer empathy, understanding, and solidarity. Sharing experiences, fears, and triumphs with others who share the same faith provides a unique bond that can be immensely comforting. ***Galatians 6:2*** encourages believers to *"carry each other's burdens, and in this way, you will fulfill the law of Christ."*

Suggestions for finding a Christian counselor or support group:

Finding a Christian counselor or support group can be an invaluable resource. To find a Christian counselor, consider reaching out to local churches, Christian organizations, or seek referral services that specialize in connecting individuals with Christian therapists. The Association of Christian Counselors (ACC), American Association of Christian Counselors (AACC), and local Christian counseling centers may provide directories or lists of professionals. These counselors are trained to integrate biblical principles with psychological techniques, providing a holistic approach to healing.

To find a support group, inquire within local churches or Christian organizations for groups specifically geared towards individuals dealing with bad memories or trauma. Online resources, such as

Christian forums or social media groups, can also be helpful in connecting with like-minded individuals seeking support.

In conclusion, seeking professional help and community support are vital aspects of overcoming bad memories. Professional therapists offer specialized guidance, utilizing therapeutic approaches suited to individual needs. Additionally, seeking support from fellow Christians provides a unique element of empathy and shared faith. By recognizing when professional help is needed and seeking support from the Christian community, individuals can effectively navigate through the healing process, finding solace and strength along the way.

Chapter VII.

Walking in Freedom from Bad Memories

To walk in freedom from bad memories, it is essential to embrace a renewed identity in Christ. This involves recognizing that our past does not define us and that through Christ, we are made new. *2 Corinthians 5:17* says, *"Therefore, if anyone is in Christ, the new creation has come: The old has gone, the new is here!"* By embracing this truth, we can let go of the labels or negative self-perceptions associated with our past and live in the freedom of our new identity in Christ.

Letting go of shame and guilt associated with bad memories:

Shame and guilt often accompany bad memories, weighing us down and hindering our progress towards healing. However, as believers, we are called to let go of shame and guilt, understanding that through Christ's sacrifice, we have been forgiven. ***Romans 8:1*** affirms this truth: *"Therefore, there is now no condemnation for those who are in Christ Jesus."* By accepting God's forgiveness and grace, we can release the burden of shame and guilt and embrace the freedom to move forward.

Living a life of purpose and joy despite past experiences:

The power of God's redemption enables us to live a life of purpose and joy, even in the face of past experiences. Despite the pain and trauma associated with bad memories, God has a plan for our lives and desires for us to experience His joy. ***Jeremiah 29:11*** declares, *"For I know the plans I have for you," declares the Lord, "plans to prosper you and not to harm you, plans to give you hope and a future."* By surrendering our past hurts to God and aligning our lives with His purposes, we can find a renewed sense of joy and fulfillment.

Encouraging others and sharing personal testimonies of healing:

One of the most powerful ways to walk in freedom from bad memories is by encouraging others and sharing our personal testimonies of healing. When we share our experiences, struggles, and victories, we provide hope and inspiration to those who may be going through similar situations. **2 Corinthians 1:4** encourages us, saying, *"He comforts us in all our troubles so that we can comfort others. When they are troubled, we will be able to give them the same comfort God has given us."* By being vulnerable and transparent, we can help others experience healing and freedom, while also strengthening our own journey.

My Testimony: Finding Joy in the Midst of Past Experiences

My name is PD John, and I want to share with you how I discovered true freedom and joy in my life, despite the bad memories that haunted me for years.

Growing up, I went through a series of painful experiences that left me feeling broken, ashamed, and filled with guilt. I carried the weight of my past like an anchor, hindering my ability to fully experience the life God had planned for me.

But one day, everything changed. I encountered God's love and forgiveness in a way I never thought possible. I discovered that through Christ, I could embrace a renewed identity. No longer was I defined by my past, but I was made new in Him.

It wasn't easy to let go of the shame and guilt that had consumed me for so long, but I found solace in **Romans 8:1,** *which reminded me that there is no condemnation for those who are in Christ Jesus. God's grace washed away the stains of my past, and I found freedom in His forgiveness.*

As I began to grasp my true identity in Christ, I realized that despite my past experiences, God had a purpose for my life. He didn't want me to continue living in the darkness of my memories;

instead, He desired to fill my life with joy and purpose.

Jeremiah 29:11 *became my guiding light, assuring me that God had plans to prosper me, give me hope, and lead me into a future filled with His goodness. I surrendered my hurts to Him, allowed Him to shape my steps, and discovered a fulfilling life that I had only dreamt of before.*

But my journey didn't end there. As I experienced healing and freedom, I felt a deep desire to share my story with others. I found solace and strength in **2 Corinthians 1:4** *which reminded me that God comforts us so that we can comfort others. I realized that my personal testimony could bring hope and encouragement to those who were going through similar struggles.*

Through vulnerability and transparency, I began to speak openly about my past, my struggles, and how God had brought me through. By doing so, I witnessed firsthand the transformative power of sharing our stories. Not only did it help others find healing, but it strengthened my own journey and deepened my relationship with God.

Today, I can confidently say that I am walking in freedom from bad memories. Though they once held me captive, I now live in the fullness of God's love, grace, and joy. Embracing my new identity in Christ, letting go of shame and guilt, living a purposeful life, and encouraging others through my testimony has truly set me free.

So, if you find yourself burdened by the weight of your past, I want to encourage you. There is hope. There is healing. And there is freedom waiting for you. Surrender your hurts to God, embrace your identity in Christ, and allow Him to lead you into a life filled with joy, purpose, and abundant blessings.

In conclusion, walking in freedom from bad memories involves embracing our identity in Christ, letting go of shame and guilt, living a purposeful and joyful life, and encouraging others through our personal testimonies. By applying these principles and seeking God's guidance, we can break free from the chains of the past and experience the fullness of the abundant life God intended for us.

Chapter VIII.

Conclusion

Recap of Key Points Discussed

Throughout this book, we have explored the powerful impact of bad memories and how they can haunt our lives. We have delved into the nature of bad memories, understanding their definition and the ways they can affect us emotionally, physically, and relationally.

Taking a biblical perspective, we have seen how God calls us to address and overcome bad memories rather than being bound by them. We have explored the importance of forgiveness, renewing our minds through Scripture, seeking healing through prayer and worship, as well as the significance of professional help and community support.

Encouragement to Continue the Journey of Healing

As we conclude this book, I want to offer you encouragement to continue the journey of healing from your bad memories. Overcoming these haunting memories is not a one-time event but rather an ongoing process. It requires perseverance, vulnerability, and a willingness to confront the pain that lies within.

It is normal to experience setbacks and moments of doubt along the way. Healing is not linear, and there may be times when old memories resurface and trigger emotions. But remember, each step forward, no matter how small, brings you closer to freedom and restoration.

Final Words of Encouragement and Empowerment from a Christian Perspective

As we part ways, I want to leave you with final words of encouragement and empowerment from a Christian perspective. Let these truths anchor your soul as you navigate the path towards overcoming bad memories:

1. Trust in God's Unfailing Love: Throughout Scripture, we are reminded of God's faithfulness in our lives. In **Psalm 91:4,** it says, *"He will cover you with his feathers, and under his wings, you will find refuge; his faithfulness will be your shield and rampart."* Lean on God's unfailing love and find solace in His presence as you journey towards healing.

2. Embrace the Power of Forgiveness: Forgiveness is a transformative act of obedience and grace. As Jesus states in **Matthew 18:21-22,** *"I tell you, not seven times, but seventy-seven times."* Just as God forgives us, we are called to extend forgiveness to others and ourselves. Embrace the freedom that comes from releasing the burden of resentment and anger.

3. Renew Your Mind with God's Truth: The power of Scripture cannot be overstated. **Romans 12:2** instructs us to *"not conform to the pattern of this world, but be transformed by the renewing of your mind."* Fill your mind with God's truth, challenge negative thought patterns, and replace them with His promises.

4. Seek Healing through Prayer and Worship: Turn to God in prayer and worship as you navigate the healing process. Pour out your heart before Him and allow His presence to bring comfort and peace. **Psalm 34:17-18** reminds us, *"The righteous cry out, and the Lord hears them; he delivers them from all their troubles. The Lord is close to the brokenhearted and saves those who are crushed in spirit."*

5. Engage in Community and Professional Support: Surround yourself with a supportive community of fellow believers who can encourage and journey with you. Seek professional help when necessary, for God works through the wisdom and expertise of counselors and therapists. **Proverbs 11:14** says, *"For lack of guidance, a nation falls, but victory is won through many advisers."*

Remember, you are not alone in this journey. God is with you, healing and restoring every area of your life. Embrace His love, trust in His plan, and press on, knowing that the journey towards overcoming bad memories is one that leads to freedom, wholeness, and a deeper relationship with our loving Creator.

May this book serve as a guide and a source of inspiration as you step into a life unburdened by the memories that once haunted you. Remember, you have a future filled with hope, joy, and purpose. Embrace it with courage and faith, for you are a beloved child of God.

Bibliography

1. Hawkins, D., (2019). Letting Go: The Pathway of Surrender. Hay House, Carlsbad.

2. Van Der Kolk, B., (2014). The Body Keeps the Score: Brain, Mind, and Body in the Healing of Trauma. Penguin Books, New York.

3. O'Connor, P., & Lader, R., (2018). Rewind, Replay, Repeat: A Memoir of Obsessive-Compulsive Disorder. University of Chicago Press, Chicago.

4. Bass, E., (2003). The Courage to Heal: A Guide for Women Survivors of Child Sexual Abuse. Harper Perennial, New York.

5. Engel, B., (2013). The Emotionally Abusive Relationship: How to Stop Being Abused and How to Stop Abusing. Adams Media, Avon.

6. Roth, G., & Heller, M., (2012). Healing Developmental Trauma: How Early Trauma Affects Self-Regulation, Self-Image, and the Capacity for Relationship. North Atlantic Books, Berkeley.

7. Neff, K., (2011). Self-Compassion: Stop Beating Yourself Up and Leave Insecurity Behind. HarperCollins, New York.

8. van der Hart, O., Nijenhuis, E., & Steele, K., (2006). The Haunted Self: Structural Dissociation and the Treatment of Chronic Traumatization. W. W. Norton & Company, New York.

9. Rothschild, B., (2000). The Body Remembers: The Psychophysiology of Trauma and Trauma Treatment. W. W. Norton & Company, New York.

10. Van Der Hart, O., & Dorahy, M., (2009). The Haunted Self: Structural Dissociation and the Treatment of Chronic Traumatization. W. W. Norton & Company, New York.

11. Herman, J., (1997). Trauma and Recovery: The Aftermath of Violence – From Domestic Abuse to Political Terror. Basic Books, New York.

12. Mate, G., (2010). In the Realm of Hungry Ghosts: Close Encounters with Addiction. North Atlantic Books, Berkeley.

OTHER BOOKS
BY PROPHET PD JOHN

1. **Level 1 Prophetic Training Manual**

Available at .Amazon.cm, Barnes & Noble, Saxo.com, Goodreads etc...

2. **Level 2 Prophetic Training Manual**

Available at .Amazon.cm, Barnes & Noble, Saxo.com, Goodreads etc...

3. Level 3 Prophetic Training Manual: Advanced Prophetic Training

Available at .Amazon.cm, Barnes & Noble, Saxo.com, Goodreads etc...

4. Level 4 Prophetic Training Manual: The Ultimate Training in Prophetic

Available at .Amazon.cm, Barnes & Noble, Saxo.com, Goodreads etc...

5. Archangel Uriel: The Keeper of Divine Light

Available at .Amazon.cm, Barnes & Noble, Saxo.com, Goodreads etc...

6. 7 Reasons Some Church Ministers Associate with Freemasons.

Available at .Amazon.cm, Barnes & Noble, Saxo.com, Goodreads etc...

7. Archangel Michael: the warrior angel,

Available at .Amazon.cm, Barnes & Noble, Saxo.com, Goodreads etc...

8.   Battle Between Godly and Satanic Altars

Available at .Amazon.cm, Barnes & Noble, Saxo.com, Goodreads etc...

9.   Dorah & The Dragons: A Fantasy Tale for Children

Available at .Amazon.cm, Barnes & Noble, Saxo.com, Goodreads etc...

10. Dreams and Interpretations: Understanding The Dream World

Available at .Amazon.cm, Barnes & Noble, Saxo.com, Goodreads etc...

11. SECRETS TO ENTER THE KINGDOM OF HEAVEN

Available at .Amazon.cm, Barnes & Noble, Saxo.com, Goodreads etc...

12. How to Meditate Effectively

Available at .Amazon.cm, Barnes & Noble, Saxo.com, Goodreads etc…

13. Mystery of Christmas Day Unveiled

Available at .Amazon.cm, Barnes & Noble, Saxo.com, Goodreads etc…

14. Train Up Your Child in the Way He Should Go

Available at .Amazon.cm, Barnes & Noble, Saxo.com, Goodreads etc...

15. Guide to Dream Journaling

Available at .Amazon.cm, Barnes & Noble, Saxo.com, Goodreads etc...

16. How to Raise the Dead

Available at .Amazon.cm, Barnes & Noble, Saxo.com, Goodreads etc...

17. How to Go Through The Process Of Spiritual Growth

18. Holy Spirity

19. How to Pray Against Monitoring Spirity

Available at .Amazon.cm, Barnes & Noble, Saxo.com, Goodreads etc...

20. Jonah The Prophet:The Burden of the Prophetic Calling

Available at .Amazon.cm, Barnes & Noble, Saxo.com, Goodreads etc...

21. Exploring The Art of Reasoning

Available at .Amazon.cm, Barnes & Noble, Saxo.com, Goodreads etc...

22. Mystery Behind Praise And Worship

Available at .Amazon.cm, Barnes & Noble, Saxo.com, Goodreads etc...

23. Level 1 Christian Seers Training Manual

Available at .Amazon.cm, Barnes & Noble, Saxo.com, Goodreads etc...

24. TITLE - LEVEL 2 CHRISTIAN SEERS TRAINING MANUAL

Available at .Amazon.cm, Barnes & Noble, Saxo.com, Goodreads etc...

25. TITLE - LEVEL 3 CHRISTIAN SEERS TRAINING MANUAL

Available at .Amazon.cm, Barnes & Noble, Saxo.com, Goodreads etc...

26. TITLE - LEVEL 4 CHRISTIAN SEERS TRAINING MANUAL: ULTIMATE TRAINING IN THE SEER MINISTRY

Available at .Amazon.cm, Barnes & Noble, Saxo.com, Goodreads etc...

27. The Azusa Street Revival: Awakening the Spirit Within

Available at .Amazon.cm, Barnes & Noble,
Saxo.com, Goodreads etc...

28. THE HEART OF A SPIRITUAL FATHER

Available at .Amazon.cm, Barnes & Noble,
Saxo.com, Goodreads etc...